Persuasion 10x

Mastering the Art of Convincing Online

A brief introduction

You know that feeling when you read a message that just grabs you and makes you want to act immediately?

Well, that's the power of persuasion! You will learn all the techniques and tricks to awaken that same reaction in people with your words.

Don't think this is something from another world, no. None of that!
I'll show you how to use the right words, create impactful sentences and structure your messages in an irresistible way.

We want you to truly connect with your target audience. This is what will make the difference when convincing them to take action.

At the heart of this strategy is the power of persuasion techniques in writing.

Influence or be Influenced

The question of wanting to influence or be influenced is a dichotomy that has permeated human interactions since time immemorial.

In an increasingly connected world, this choice has become more evident and relevant than ever. In a society that values individuality, authenticity and the ability to shape your own destiny, influence plays a central role in our lives, affecting our decisions, opinions and behaviors.

I want to show you how explore the complexities of influence and the desire to be influenced, considering the different aspects of this dynamic in the personal, social and digital spheres. Let's examine the motivations behind both sides of the coin, the benefits and drawbacks of each choice, and how this relates to identity construction and impact on society.

The Quest for Power and Change

Influencing, in essence, involves the ability to affect the opinions, decisions and actions of other people. It can be seen as an act of leadership, where someone uses their knowledge, charisma and persuasive skills to guide others towards certain goals or ideals. Those who want to influence often crave power and have a specific vision of the world they want to create.

Motivations for wanting to influence can vary widely. Some individuals seek influence as a form of personal power, seeking to gain an advantage over others or achieve ambitious goals. Others have more altruistic motivations, wanting to use their influence to make positive changes in society by promoting social or environmental causes.

Personal Power: For many, influence is a tool to gain personal power and achieve their goals. This may include influencing people in positions of authority, such as political leaders or company executives, to make decisions that benefit their interests. The desire to influence may be motivated by personal ambition, greed, or the desire for control.

Social Change: On the other hand, many individuals want to influence to bring about positive changes in society. This may involve advocating for causes such as gender equality, racial justice, environmental preservation, or poverty eradication. Those who seek influence for altruistic reasons often want to see a better world and are willing to use their influence to make a difference.

Influencing positively can bring a series of benefits to both the influencer and those being influenced.

Goal Achievement: The ability to influence can help individuals achieve their personal and professional goals. It can be a valuable tool for advancing your career, ensuring business success, or gaining needed support for important social causes.

Positive Change: Influence can also be used to bring about positive changes in society. Those who have the ability to influence can help create a more just, equal and sustainable world by making a difference on critical issues.

Self-Esteem and Recognition: Being able to influence others often leads to an increase in self-esteem and social recognition. People who are successful at influencing are often admired and respected for their leadership ability.

Being Influenced: The Search for Identification and Connection On the other hand, being influenced implies being willing to listen, learn and be shaped by other people, ideas or trends. This can be seen as a demonstration of humility and openness to change. Those who choose to be influenced often seek identification, belonging, and guidance.

Motivations to Be Influenced

The reasons for choosing to be influenced can be equally diverse. Some individuals value the perspective and wisdom of others, seeking to learn and grow through the influence of mentors, leaders, or inspirational figures. Others may be influenced by social pressure or the desire to fit into a certain group or culture.

Learning and Growth: For many, being influenced is an effective way to learn and grow. By absorbing knowledge and perspectives from other people, you can broaden your horizons, acquire new skills, and improve as an individual.

Identification and Belonging: Being influenced can also provide a sense of identification and belonging. Many seek influence to feel connected to a specific group, culture or community. This may be especially relevant in a world where identity and acceptance play an important role.

Choosing to be influenced can also bring a series of benefits to an individual's life.

Continuous Learning: By being open to influence, you can continue learning throughout your life, acquiring new knowledge and skills that can be applied in different areas.

Social Connection: Being influenced often leads to greater social connection. By aligning yourself with influential ideas or groups, you can develop meaningful relationships and find a sense of belonging.

Flexibility and Adaptability: The ability to be influenced also demonstrates flexibility and adaptability, valuable characteristics in an ever-changing world. Those who are willing to adapt to new ideas and perspectives are better prepared to face challenges and excel.

In modern society, the choice between influencing or being influenced is not always clear or static. In many cases, people switch between these two positions depending on the context and circumstances. Furthermore, the line between influence and being influenced often becomes blurred as social, cultural and digital interactions intertwine.

Digital Influence and Social Networks

One of the main drivers of this complexity is the rise of social media and digital influence. Platforms like Facebook, Instagram, Twitter and YouTube have given anyone with access to the internet the ability to influence and be influenced on a global scale. Digital influencers, in particular, have become prominent figures, shaping the opinions and behaviors of millions of followers.

Digital Influence: Those who choose to be influenced often do so by following digital influencers whose lives and opinions can serve as a source of inspiration or entertainment. Digital influencers have the ability to create trends, promote products and even affect social change.

Being Negatively Influenced: However, digital influence can also have negative effects, especially among younger people. The pressure to conform to unrealistic beauty standards, the search for validation on social media and exposure to hate speech are examples of how harmful digital influence can be.

Influencing on Social Media: On the other hand, many individuals use social media platforms to express their opinions, promote causes, and build online communities. Those looking to influence can leverage these platforms to reach a broad audience and mobilize support for their causes.

Identity and Authenticity

Another important aspect to be considered when choosing between influencing and being influenced is the construction of identity and the search for authenticity. In a world where individuality is valued, the pressure to be authentic while still fitting into social and cultural norms can be challenging.

Identity Construction: Many individuals choose to be influenced in the search for models to follow in the construction of their identity. They may draw inspiration from public figures, spiritual leaders, or other role models.

Authenticity Challenge: On the other hand, the pressure to be influential can create a challenge to authenticity. Some may be tempted to shape their identities according to the expectations of others rather than remaining true to themselves.

Moral Responsibility

The choice between influencing and being influenced is also intrinsically linked to moral responsibility. Those who wish to influence have a responsibility to use their influence ethically and responsibly, considering the impact of their actions on others and society as a whole.

Influencer Responsibility: Influencers have the power to shape the opinions and behaviors of their followers, and this influence must be used responsibly. Promoting false information, inciting hatred or exploiting people's vulnerabilities are examples of behaviors that can be harmful.

Conscious Choice: Those who choose to be influenced also have a responsibility to make conscious choices about who and what they follow. Blindly believing information or following harmful influencers without question can have negative consequences.

The choice between influencing or being influenced is a decision that everyone faces in their lives, and often, this choice is not definitive. Modern society presents a complex web of influences, from personal interactions to the constantly evolving digital world. Both options have their motivations, benefits and challenges.

The important thing is to recognize the complexity of this dynamic and make choices that contribute to personal growth, social well-being and the construction of a more just and egalitarian world.

A curious question…

Do you know what the most valuable skill in the world is?

Simple: the ability to sell.

Not just products and services, but ideas, concepts and beliefs.

Maybe you know it or not, but power goes to those who are persuasive, and this is true for every business in every country in the world.

It's important that you have a way to convince people (your boss, colleagues, clients, investors, etc.) that your ideas (and your work) are worth it.

I've identified some fundamental selling secrets over the years – some tricks of the trade. And that's exactly what I'm going to share with you now – the foundations behind every great sales piece.

I call them THE THREE FUNDAMENTAL RULES OF SELLING

and they are…

#1. People don't like the idea that they are being sold to.

#2. People buy things for emotional reasons, not rational ones.

#3. Once they are bought in, people need to excuse their emotional decisions with logic.

Let's see **rule #1**: People don't like being sold to them. At first, this doesn't make sense. Every year, trillions of dollars worth of goods and services are bought and sold... billions through the Post Office alone. Think about your friends. Many of them undoubtedly love to shop.

People like to buy things, but they don't like to be sold to them. Remember this. Whether you're writing a sales letter or trying to convince your friend to go to a concert, don't put pressure on them. Offer to give something. Don't force it, try.

Let's say you want to get your friend to buy a piece of chocolate cake. You wouldn't start by listing the 10 reasons why cake is good for him, right? Of course not.

In real life, if you really wanted to get a friend to buy a piece of cake, you would probably start by describing how good the cake smells, how wet it is, how much frosting it has, and how it will melt in your mouth.
In other words, you would create a verbal image that triggers your desires – your hunger, your desire for chocolate. You would tempt him by appealing to his emotions. You wouldn't bore him with reasons or force him.

Understand this first principle and you will have people eating out of your hand.

Rule #2 Hit where it hurts: People buy things for emotional reasons, not rational ones.

If people acted rationally, you couldn't sell chocolate cake.

There is no logical reason to eat it. It's not nutritious. Get fat. It kills the metabolism. And it's expensive.

So why is chocolate cake a multi-million dollar industry?

Because it makes you feel good!

To be persuasive, you need to focus on your prospect's feelings and desires.

See seven important ones: fear, greed, vanity, lust, pride, envy and laziness.

Rule #3: Once the prospect has already bought emotionally, he needs to justify his irrational decision with rational reasons.

Now, you are ready to understand what copywriting is.

Copywriting

There is no way to talk about persuasion in the digital age without mentioning the famous Copywriting (or copy). This is one of the most essential elements of marketing.

It is the art and science of strategically delivering words (whether written or spoken) that makes people take action.

Nothing is more persuasive than someone who knows how to use words. If used well, they are capable of making someone make an instant decision. This is real Copywriting!

How copywriting came about

If you think that Copywriting emerged today, you are wrong.

The first time the word "copy" was used was in the 19th century, in 1828.

Noah Webster, an American dictionary, defined copy as "an authorial creation to be imitated, both in writing and in printing."

But the definition fell into disuse for years and only resurfaced in 1870, when it began to describe professionals who wrote advertisements, differentiating themselves from traditional copywriters.

During the 19th century and the entire 20th century, the persuasive writing of Copywriters was used mainly in advertising writing.

The advancement of the internet and the growth of Digital Marketing meant that Copywriting adopted a particular identity, reformulated and far from advertising.

The mess they made with advertising

Tell me something, what is advertising for you?

Is it something to be considered as work or as a work of art?

Are they clever slogans or entertaining prose?

Is it a work to be judged for an award or recognition?

I'll tell you, it's none of the options above.

Advertising is a multiplied seller.
Just it.

And written advertising, or copywriting, is an art of selling whether on paper or digitally.

The purpose of a copywriter's work is to sell. Full stop.

The sale is made by persuading with the written word, in the same way that a television commercial sells (*if done correctly of course*), persuading with visual and audio effects.

Just as Claude Hopkins wrote in his timeless classic, Scientific Advertising:

"To correctly understand advertising or even to learn its rudiments one must begin with correct perception.

Advertising is the art of selling. Its principles are the principles of the art of selling. The successes and failures in both lines are due to similar causes.

Therefore, each advertising question must be answered by the seller's standards.

Let's emphasize this point. The sole purpose of advertising is to make sales.

It is not to give a general impression. It's not about putting your name in front of people. It's not primarily made to help sellers. Treat her like a salesman.

It justifies itself.

Compare it with other sellers.

Record your costs and results.

Don't accept any excuses because good salespeople don't make them. And so you won't be far wrong.

Advertising is a multiplied seller. It can appeal to thousands while a salesperson only speaks to one person. This is a corresponding cost.

Some people spend an average of 10 dollars per word on an ad. Therefore, all ads must be a super seller.

A seller's mistake can cost little. An advertiser's mistake can cost a thousand times more. Therefore, be more cautious and more demanding. A mediocre salesperson can affect a small part of your business. Mediocre advertising affects your entire business.

These points are as true today as they were when they were written almost a hundred years ago!

So the goal becomes: how can we make our advertising as effective as possible.

The answer is to test. Test again. And then test some more.

If ad "A" receives a two percent response rate, and ad "B" receives three percent, then we can deduce that ad "B" will continue to outperform ad "A."
But testing takes time, and can be expensive if not kept under control. Therefore, it is ideal to start with some proven ads, tested and known ideas and work from there.

For example, if tests have shown over decades or more that targeted advertising significantly outperforms non-targeted advertising, then we can start with that assumption and work from there.

If we know based on test results that making an ad that speaks directly to an individual works better than facing the masses, then it makes little sense to start testing with the assumption that this doesn't happen.

This is common sense.

So it's logical to know some basic rules or techniques about efficient writing. Test results will always be the ultimate asset, but it's best to have a starting point before testing.

So this starting point is the essence of this book.
The tips, expressed here, have generally been tested over time and known to be effective.

But I can't emphasize enough that when using these techniques, you should always test them before launching a large, expensive campaign.

Sometimes a small change here or there is all that's needed to increase response rates dramatically.

And with that, let's move on........

Focus on them,

And Not On You

When a prospect reads your ad, post, letter, etc., the only thing they will be asking themselves from the beginning is: "what's in it for me?"

And if your text doesn't tell him anything, it will end up in the trash faster than he can read the title.

Many advertisers make this mistake. They focus on them as a company.

How long have they been open, who are their biggest customers, who already has ten years of research and millions of dollars in product development, blah, blah.
Indeed, these points are important.

But they must be expressed in a way that interests your potential customer. Remember, once the ad is trashed, the sale is lost!

When writing your texts, it helps to think of them as a letter written to an old friend. In fact, I often imagine a friend of mine who best fits the profile of my prospects. What would I say to convince my friend to try my product?

How can I segment my friend's objections and beliefs to help me?

When you're writing to a friend, you'll use the pronouns "I" and "you." When trying to convince your friend, you could say, "Look, I know you think you've tried every gadget out there. But you should know that..."

And this goes beyond just writing in the second person. In other words, treat your prospects as "you" in your texts. The fact is that there are many successful ads that are not written in the second person.

Some are written in the first-person perspective, where the writer uses "I." Other times, the third person is used, such as "she," "he," and "they."

And even if you write in the second person, it doesn't necessarily mean your copy is about them.

For example:

"Being a real estate agent, you can take comfort in the fact that I have sold over 10,000 homes and have mastered the tricks of the trade."

Even though you are writing in the second person, you are still focusing on yourself.

So how can you focus on them?

I'm glad you asked.

One of the ways is...

Stages of Consumer Consciousness

Awareness level here basically means whether the potential customer is aware of your product or whether they are aware that there is a solution to their problem.

Knowing exactly where it is will determine the type of content you write.

Figuring this out can increase conversions 2X or more.

Legendary copywriter Gene Schwartz gave the following rule:

If the potential customer is already familiar with the product and knows it can help them, the title should start with the product. If your avatar doesn't know your product but has a desire, you lead with that desire.

Finally, if the prospect doesn't really know what they need, but just has a general problem, you start with the problem and write the copy to make the prospect realize they need your solution.

These are the basics. Gene established 5 levels of customer awareness that explain this concept in more detail, and that's what I'm going to get into now.

So, your 5 levels of customer knowledge are:

Level 1 - is the most attentive customer – this person knows what they want, trusts you, and when you offer something new, there is a good chance they will buy it. These customers are what every marketer wants. For example, think about brands that have a following like Nike and Apple.
The consumer knows the brand and wants the product, there is no effort at the time of sale.

Level 2 - product aware. These people don't trust you yet – they know you're selling something they want, but they're not sure if it's right for them. Since they don't yet trust you, they read reviews, look at testimonials, and try to determine if your product can do what you say. With prospects like these, the goal of your copy should be to immediately reassure them. These first two categories, by the way, are the easiest to make sales. As your avatar becomes less aware, you have a harder job ahead of you.

Alright, the next level of customer awareness is solution awareness.

Level 3 - These are people who have a problem, they know there is a solution to it, but they don't know your product and the results they can get with it. With prospects like these, you want them to know that you understand their desires and that your product will help them get there.

As we move more towards awareness, we start to reach those potential customers who can really help your business grow. So the next type of customer awareness is problem awareness.

Level 4 - This is someone who is worried – he feels like he has a problem, but he doesn't know there is a solution to it. With this type of customer, you want your lead to show them that you understand their frustration and anxiety.
Finally, there is the completely unconscious client.

Level 5 – These people are hard to sell to. They don't realize they have a problem, they don't know anything about your brand and they don't even know there is a solution to what they are experiencing. With this type of person, you will have to present a powerful and extremely irresistible offer. You need to present your offer as if it were a drawing, where people can see all the details, even see the colors, smell, taste and texture of what you are offering.

Understanding and adapting to different levels of consumer awareness is key to building an effective marketing strategy.

By adjusting your message, approach and tactics according to the stage the consumer is at, you can increase the chances of engagement, conversion and loyalty.

By taking the 5 levels of consumer awareness into consideration, you will be better prepared to meet your target audience's needs, make a meaningful connection, and build lasting relationships.

Deepen your knowledge of consumer behavior, research and test your strategies and always be willing to adapt to changes and market demands. This way you will be on the right path to success in your marketing and sales initiatives.

Additionally, remember that consumers can move between different levels of consciousness over time.

They can start at the level of unconsciousness and, through information and interactions, progress to the following stages.

Therefore, it's essential to keep a close eye on your target audience's behavior so you can adjust your strategy as needed.

Another important point to consider is the importance of clear and consistent communication at each stage of consciousness.

Whether through educational content, storytelling, testimonials or product demonstrations, it is essential to convey your message in an effective and relevant way.

By doing this, you will be nurturing consumer trust and creating an emotional connection with your brand.

How to highlight the benefits

And the what are the characteristics?

They are descriptions of the qualities that a product possesses.

• Car XYZ gets 55 kilometers per liter in the city

• Frame is made from a lightweight and durable steel.

• Our glue is protected by a patent.

• This database has an internal data search system.

But what are the benefits?

Well, they are what results mean to your potential customers.

• You'll save money on gas and reduce environmental
pollutants when you use our high-performance energy-efficient

hybrid car. Plus, you'll feel the extra power when you're passing other cars, it's courtesy of the efficient electric motor, which they don't have!

• Lightweight alloy-durable steel frame means you'll be able to take it with ease, and use it in places other ladders can't go, while also supporting up to 800 pounds. No back pain when dragging a heavy ladder. And since it will last 150 years, you will never need to buy another ladder again!

• Patented glue ensures you can use it on wood, plastic, ceramics, metal, glass and tile... without difficult cleaning and without having to re-glue - guaranteed!

• You can instantly see the "big picture" hidden in your data, and pull out the more arcane statistics whenever you want.

Watch your business do a "180" quickly, so you instantly know what's failing!

It's all done with our data search system which is so easy to use, my twelve year old son used it successfully as soon as he started using it.

I created these examples, but I think you understand what I mean.

NOTE: you are not writing to impress your Portuguese teacher or win a prize.

The only prize you want to win is for your text to sell and beat your best previous ad, and at the same time to have some freedom in grammar, punctuation and sentence structure. You want it to be read and people to act on, not read and admired!

But back to the benefits…

If you were selling an expensive watch, you wouldn't tell your reader that the watch's cover is 5 inches in diameter and the strap is made of leather.

You should show him how the extra-large display will tell you the time in the blink of an eye. Ahhh yes!

He doesn't want to have to look for the time on the clock and look foolish in front of everyone around him trying to read this magnificent clock.

And how about the way he projects success and charisma when he wears the gold watch with its beautiful custom crafted leather strap?

How irresistible your love will find you when he's all dressed up to go out, wearing his watch. Or how the status and beauty of the watch will attract the ladies.

By the way, did you notice that I highlighted that seeing well is a benefit?

Does this seem like a silly benefit?

Not if you are selling to baby boomers who suffer from degraded vision.

They probably hate it when someone they're trying to impress sees them squinting and trying to read something.

It's all about your inner desires, that's what you need to discover. And that even they may not even know.

That is…until you show them a better way.

The point here is to address the benefits of the product, not its features. And when you do that, you're focusing on your reader and their interests, their desires.

The trick is to highlight the specific benefits that press your reader's emotional buttons.

How do you do it?

I'll show!

The Big Idea and the Rule of One

Whenever the subject is copywriting, the concept of the "Big Idea" comes to the fore. David Ogilvy talks about him and several other authors, such as Michael Masterson and John Forde, authors of the book Great Leads, as well.

The concept is quite simple, but a lot of people make bad mistakes.

Basically, the Big Idea, or Rule of One, proposes that your text focuses on just one action, one promise, one idea that must be objective and without "accessories".

I'll put some examples here for you to compare and understand the difference from the Big Idea.

Examples without the Big Idea:

Lists (161 New Ways to Win a Man's Heart...);

Generic plurals (The Crimes We Commit Against Our Stomachs)

Examples with the Big Idea:

Specific (The Secret to Making People Like You);

Targeted (To Men Who Want to Quit One Day);

Impact (Is a Child's Life Worth $1 to You?).

Despite being somewhat appealing examples (taken from the book Great Leads), the difference between the Big Idea in these titles is clear, isn't it?

Can you tell what the focal point of the first two examples is? It's difficult to say, since they are quite broad and unfocused.

However, examples using the Big Idea framework are much more focused.

Therefore, we can say with confidence about the subject they introduce, even if we have no knowledge about the product to which they are linked.

So, be very clear about your Big Idea. To do this, you must work with the following structure:

A good idea: show the benefits or advantages of the product/solution you are selling;

A core emotion: create a connection with the reader, provoking engagement through emotional reinforcement so that the rational continues to progress in the text;

A captivating story: reinforces the central emotion. It is often a case, an episode or brings data and figures that prove your offer (product/service);

A unique and desirable benefit: consolidates the advantage (benefit) that your product or service offers the reader;

An inevitable answer: point out the path that must be followed for your reader to reach the benefit you are talking about.

This is all so that we can support the title from an introduction (called, in this context, a lead) that must use the correct technique, depending on the reader's level of awareness.

This technique can be a story, a prediction, a declaration, a promise, etc.).

Regardless of which one you use, it is important that your single Big Idea is supported by an equally unique emotion, to direct the reader towards the desired action.

Pressing Emotional Buttons

This is where research really pays off. Because, to press the buttons, you first need to know what they are.

Watch this story, and you will understand what I want to tell you: once upon a time there was a young man who walked into a certain Chevrolet dealership to see a Chevy Camaro.

He had money, and was ready to make a purchasing decision. But he couldn't decide whether he wanted to buy the Camaro or the Ford Mustang when he was on his way to the Ford dealership.

A salesman approached him and quickly discovered the man's dilemma.

"Tell me what you like most about the Camaro," the salesman said.

"It's a fast car. I like its speed."

After some discussion, the salesman learned that the man had started dating a college cheerleader.

So what did the seller do?

Simple. He changed his speech and thus hit emotional buttons, because he knew it would help promote the sale.

He told the man that his new girlfriend would be impressed when he came home with this car!

He put the mental image in the man's mind that he and his girlfriend were traveling to the beach in the Camaro.

And how jealous all his friends would be when they see him driving around with a pretty girl in a nice car.

And suddenly the man had the vision. He got it. And the seller saw this and worked on this point. And before you know it, the man writes the Chevrolet dealership a nice check!

The salesman found the emotional buttons and pushed them like never before until the man realized he wanted the Camaro more than he wanted his money.

I know what you're thinking... the man said he liked the car because it was fast, didn't he?
Yes that was it. But subconsciously, what he really wanted was a car that would impress his girlfriend, his friends, and in his mind make them like him even more! In his mind, he equates speed with excitement.

Not because he wanted an endless amount of speeding tickets, but because he thought the thrill would make him more attractive, and more likable.

Perhaps the man did not even realize this fact. But the seller noticed. And he knew which emotional buttons he had to press to get the sale.

Now, why does research pay off?

Well, a good salesperson knows how to ask the questions that will tell you which buttons to press quickly. When you're writing sales copy, you don't have that luxury.

Therefore, for this very reason, it is very important to know your customers' wants, needs and desires in advance.

If you haven't done your homework, your prospect will decide they'd rather keep their money with you than buy your product.

Remember, copywriting is salesmanship on paper or digitally!

It's been said many times: People don't like to be sold.

But they like to buy.

And they buy first and foremost based on emotion.

They then justify their decision with logic, even after they have already been emotionally sold. So don't forget to support your emotional speech with logic to nourish the justification in the end.

And while we're on the subject, let's talk a little about exaggerations on sales pages. Many "conservative" marketers have decided that they don't like exaggeration, because they consider exaggeration to be "old style", they've done it, and they think that customers won't fall for it, it's no longer credible.

What they must understand is that it is not the exaggerations themselves that do not sell well.

Some less experienced copywriters often try to compensate for their lack of research or not fully understanding their target market or their own product by adding tons of adjectives, adverbs and exclamation marks and lots of bold type.

Really! If you do your job, this is not necessary.

That's not to say that some adverbs or adjectives don't have their place... only if they're used sparingly, and only if they move toward selling.

I think you'll agree that supporting your texts with evidence and credibility will go much further in convincing your potential customers than using "power words" alone.

I say power words because there are certain adjectives and adverbs that have been proven to make a difference when they are included.

This in itself is not an exaggeration. But repeated many times, they become less effective.

Which brings us to our next tip...

There will always be objections

Objections are psychological barriers that arise in consumers' minds, generating resistance to the offers presented.

Understanding objections and being able to overcome them is essential to increasing the conversion rate and boosting the success of marketing campaigns.

The Nature of Objections

It is important to recognize that objections are a natural defensive response on the part of consumers. In an increasingly saturated market with a large volume of information, consumers are increasingly cautious about their purchasing decisions.

Purchasing a product or service is seen as an investment, and it is natural for people to have doubts and concerns before committing.

Identifying Objections

To overcome objections, it is essential to identify them clearly and precisely.

By analyzing interactions with your target audience, whether through surveys, feedback or data analysis, it is possible to identify the main concerns and resistance that consumers present in relation to your offers. This allows you to understand the underlying reason behind these objections and find effective ways to overcome them.

Addressing Objections

When addressing objections, it is crucial to convey confidence and offer relevant information that dispels the public's concerns.

Objection busting involves providing solid, persuasive arguments that demonstrate the value and benefits of your offering while respecting consumers' legitimate concerns.

An effective strategy for overcoming objections is to anticipate them. When developing your marketing content, whether in ads, emails or sales pages, you can anticipate the most common objections and proactively address them. This involves providing information that combats concerns before they even arise in consumers' minds.

When responding to objections, it is important to use an empathetic and personalized approach.

Show that you understand your target audience's concerns and provide clear, relevant information that dispels them.

Use real examples, testimonials from satisfied customers, and case studies to demonstrate how your offering overcomes objections and meets consumer needs.

Another effective strategy is offering guarantees and extra benefits that reduce the risk perceived by the consumer.

Offering a satisfaction guarantee, a free trial period, or an exclusive bonus can help reassure consumers and encourage them to overcome their objections and take the desired action.

Additionally, creating a sense of urgency can also be effective in breaking down objections. By offering limited-time promotions or highlighting limited availability of the product or service, you create a sense of urgency that motivates consumers to take action. This feeling of scarcity can be a determining factor in overcoming objections, as consumers fear losing the opportunity if they don't act immediately.

It is essential to highlight the competitive differentiators of your product or service when addressing objections. Show how you stand out from the competition and offer unique solutions to your target audience's problems and needs. By highlighting the strengths of your offer, you are providing clear reasons for consumers to overcome their objections and choose your brand.

Transparency is essential in overcoming objections. Be honest about the limitations or challenges of your offering, but also highlight the benefits and solutions it provides. Honesty generates trust and credibility, key elements for overcoming consumer objections.

It is important to emphasize that objection breaking is not about manipulation or aggressive persuasion. The goal is to provide relevant information, answer legitimate questions, and help consumers make informed decisions. The focus should be on building long-term relationships and providing value to customers, rather than just seeking a quick sale.

By identifying the most common objections, anticipating them, and addressing them in an empathetic and persuasive way, you'll be on your way to earning your target audience's trust and motivating them to take action.

Finally, always be willing to listen to consumer feedback and adapt your strategies according to their needs and concerns. Constantly perfecting your objection-busting techniques will help you stand out in the market, earn consumers' trust, and achieve positive, lasting results.

Incorporating Proof and Credibility

When your prospect reads your ad, you want to make sure they believe every claim you make about your product or service. Because if there's any doubt in his mind, he won't bite, no matter how sweet the deal is.

In fact, the "too good to be true" mentality will practically guarantee a lost sale... even if it's all true.

So what can you do to increase perceived credibility?

Because after all, it's the perception you need to resolve.

But of course you must also make sure that your text is accurate and truthful.

Here are some tried and true methods that will help:

• If you are dealing with your existing customers who already know that you deliver what you promise, it emphasizes that trust. Don't let them figure it out. Make them stop, nod their heads, and say, "Yes. ABC Company has never hurt me before. I can trust them."

• Include testimonials from satisfied customers. Don't forget to include full and local names whenever possible.
Remember, "José" is much less convincing than "Armando Soares, Rio De Janeiro, Brazil." You can also include a photo of the client and/or a professional title, which is even better.
It doesn't matter if your testimonials aren't from someone famous or that your prospect doesn't know these people personally.

If you have sufficiently convincing testimonials, and they are credible, you are doing a much better job than if you don't include them.

• Pepper your texts with facts and research findings to support your claims. Be sure to source all information, even if the fact is common knowledge, as a neutral source does not give much credibility.

• In direct offer letters or certain advertisements where the texts are in the form of a letter from a specific individual, it helps to include a photo of that person.

But unlike "traditional" real estate industry letters and other similar advertisements, I would place the photo at the end of the letter, near your signature, or in the middle of the copy, rather than at the top because it will detract from your title.

And...if your sales letter is from a specific individual, be sure to include their credentials establishing them as an expert in their field (related to your product or service, of course).

• If applicable, cite any awards or third-party reviews that the third-party product or service has received.

• If you sold a lot of products, tell them. It's the old saying "10 million people can't be wrong" (those 10 million might be wrong, but your prospect will probably side with you on this one).

• Include a return policy and make it clear! It's just good business policy. Often times, offering a double money-back guarantee for certain products will result in higher profits.

Yes, you will get more refunds, but if you sell three times as many products as before, and only have to refund twice as much as before, it could be worth it, depending on your offer and return on investment.

Crunch the numbers and see what makes sense. Most importantly, test! Make them think: "Wow, they wouldn't be so generous with returns if it wasn't really what they were promising about their product!"

• If you can add a celebrity endorsement, it helps establish credibility. Wow, if Pelé recommends your product and supports what you promise, it must be true! .

• When it makes sense, use third-party testimonials. What are third party testimonials? Here are some examples from some websites I wrote when I didn't have many customer testimonials yet.

"Spyware, without any doubt, has seen an exponential increase in the last six months."
- Alfred Huger, Director of Engineering, Symantec Security Response (maker of Norton security software)

"Just click on a banner and you can install spyware."
- Dave Methvin, Chief Technology Officer, PC Pitstop

One deployment method is to "trick users into consenting to download software that they think is absolutely necessary" - Paul Bryan, director of Security and Technology Unit, Microsoft.

Did you see what I did?

I used quotes from experts in their respective fields and transformed them for my purposes.

But be sure to obtain your consent or permission from the copyright holder, if there is any need to use copyrighted materials ask about their source.

Note that I also pressed an emotional button: fear.

It has been proven that people generally do more to avoid pain than to obtain pleasure.

So why not use this tidbit of information to your advantage?

• Reveal a flaw in your product. This helps alleviate the "too good to be true" syndrome.

Reveal a flaw that isn't really a flaw. Or reveal a flaw that is minor, just to show that you are being open, about your product's shortcomings.

example:

"You're probably thinking now that this tennis racket is a miracle - and it is. But I must tell you that it has a small defect.

My racket takes about 2 weeks to get used to.

In fact, once you start using it, your game will actually get worse. But if you continue to use it, you will see a tremendous improvement in your serves, net play, and so on.

There is a tendency to think, with all the ads we are bombarded with these days, that each advertiser is always showing only what is best. And I think this line of reasoning is open-ended.

But isn't it refreshing when someone stands out from the crowd and is honest? In other words, the reader will start to subconsciously believe that you are revealing all the flaws.

• Use "complimentary notes" These brief notes are from a person in authority. Not necessarily from a celebrity, although it can also add credibility.

A person of authority is someone recognized in their field (which is related to your product) and who is qualified to speak. Complimented notes can be distributed as inserts, on a separate page, or even as part of the text. As always, test!

• If you are limiting the offer with a deadline that ends on a certain date, make sure the deadline is real and does not change. Deadlines that change every day reduce credibility.

The prospect will be suspicious "if the deadline keeps changing, he's not telling the truth... I wonder what else he's not telling the truth about."

• Avoid "exaggerations". Unfounded that I discussed in my previous tip. Enough said.

The Unique Value Proposition

The PUV is often one of the most misunderstood elements of a good sales letter.

It's what separates your product or service from your competitors. Let's take a quick look at some unique selling propositions for a product;

1) Lowest Price - If you have your business in the area of cheap prices, flaunt it. Wal-Mart has made this PUV famous lately, but it's not new to them.

Selling cheaper has been used for as long as capitalism. I don't like price wars, because someone can come along and sell it cheaper.

So it's time for a new strategy.

2) Superior Quality- If it outperforms your competitor's product or is made with high-quality materials, it's a good bet you'll use this fact to your advantage.

For example, compare your product to your competitors. From the superior packaging to the healthy ingredients, the quality is evident. It may cost a little more than your competitor, but for your market, it sells.

3) Service - If you offer superior service compared to your competitor, people will buy from you. This is especially true in certain markets that are very service-related: long distance, Internet providers, cable television, etc.

4) Exclusive Rights – My favorite! If you can legitimately claim that your product is protected by a patent or copyright, licensing agreement, etc., then you have an exclusive right as a winner. If you have a patent, even the President has to buy it from you.

Okay, isn't your product or service different from your competitor? I disagree, because there are always differences. The trick is to turn them into a positive advantage for you. So what can we do about this scenario?

One way is to present something that your company has developed internally that no other company does.

Look, there's a reason why the computer at store "A" offers to beat its competitors' price for the same product by X.

If you look closely, the two packages are never exactly the same. Company "B" offers a free scanner, while company "A" offers a printer. Or some other difference. They are comparing apples to oranges.

So unless you find a company with the exact same package (you won't.. they studied this), you won't be able to win the promotion.

But what if you actually have the same device to sell as the guy across the street?

Unless your prospect knows the inner workings of both your product and your competitor's, including the manufacturing process, customer service, and everything in between, then you potentially have license for a little creativity. But you must be truthful.

For example, if I tell my readers that my product is steam bathed to ensure purity and cleanliness (like cans and bottles in most beer brewing processes), it doesn't matter that John's beer across the street does the same. thing.

The fact that John does not announce this fact makes him hisunique product in the eyes of your prospect.

Want more examples of PUV?

• We are the only auto repair shop that will buy your car if you are not 100 percent satisfied with our work.
• Delivered in 30 minutes or it's on us!
• No furniture company will pay for your transportation.
• Our recipe is so secret that only three people in the world know it!

As with most ways to increase response, research is key with your UPV. Sometimes your PUV is obvious, for example when you have a patent. Other times you must do a little research work to discover it (or tailor it to your target market).

This is where a little persistence really pays off.

Let me give an example to illustrate what I mean:

Suppose your company sells bean bag chairs for children. So you, being the wise marketer that you are, decide to sell the puffs to prospects before writing your sales copy.

After you've given about twenty different sales presentations for your product, you discover that 75 percent of the people you spoke to asked if the puffs would eventually leak.

Since bean bags are for kids, it's only logical that parents are worried about their young ones jumping on them, rolling on them, and doing every possible thing to break the stitching and deflate the bean bag.

So when you write your text, you make sure to address this question: "You can be assured that our super-strong beanbags are triple-stitched for guaranteed leak-proof performance. No other company will do this guarantee on your puffs!

THE UNIQUE MECHANISM

This is the most important point in your marketing and, perhaps, in your life. If you master it, chances are you'll never need to worry about the competition again.

Have you ever stopped to think about how many products similar to yours exist? How many people with skills similar to yours are out there?

What will be the secret, then, for a few people and products to stand out? The answer is: the single mechanism.

Yes, it is a mechanism. It is not a point, it is not a sentence, but rather an operating scheme capable of bringing the solution to another, in the simplest, most effective and different way than anything that has ever been seen.

To illustrate, let's look at something very common... frying pans.

But what do frying pans have to do with my business? ALL!

You can find frying pans for R$40.00. However, many people have already been tempted to purchase the Polishop frying pan (if they haven't already)... the one that costs more than R$200.00 and you see on TV. If you haven't seen it yet, I recommend you watch it.

Oh, and no, it doesn't stand out because "it's on TV". After all, you ignore hundreds of other commercials...

This is just a clear example. But all the big businesses I've seen to date have a unique mechanism for their products and services, even if you don't see it as clearly as Polishop does. All the people who get the best jobs in companies sell themselves with a unique mechanism.

Therefore, if you want to stand out, avoid the fight for prices and awaken the desire of others, answer 3 questions:

- Why does my product/service solve people's problems?

- How does my product/service lead people to the success they see?

- What differentiates my product/service from everything else out there?

Believe me, it works from markets with little competition to the most competitive ones. In fact, it is completely ethical, if you only work with the truth.

I myself have created dozens of mechanisms for the weight loss sector, for example, which is currently an extremely competitive sector as well as being very delicate because we are talking about health.

The key to the mechanism is KNOWING that you are UNIQUE (we all are, no matter how much some try to say that we are replaceable) and highlighting your strengths.

HEADLINE

If you're going to make a single change to increase your response rate, focus on your title (*You have one, don't you?*).

Why? Because there will be five times more people reading the title than your text. Quite simply, a headline... is an ad for your ad.

People won't stop their busy lives to read your text unless you give them a good reason to do so.

So, a good title promises some news and a benefit.

Maybe you're thinking, "What's this new story?"

Think about the last time you "browsed" through your local newspaper.

You've skimmed through the articles one by one, and occasionally an ad may have grabbed your attention. Which ads were most likely to catch your attention?

The ones that looked like an article, of course.
Those with a title that promise news.

Those with font types that closely resembled the font types used in articles.

The ones that were placed where the articles were placed (instead of being placed on a page full of advertisements, for example).

And those with the most attractive titles that convince you that the text is worth a few minutes to read.

The title is therefore powerful and important.

I've seen many ads over the years that don't even have a title. And that's nonsense. It's the equivalent of throwing away good money spent on advertising.

Why? Because your response can increase dramatically, not by adding a headline, but by making that headline almost irresistible to your target audience.

And those last three words are important. "Your target audience".

For example. Take a look at the following title:

Announcing... New Cutting-Edge Technology Gloves That Protect Against Hazardous Waste.

News, and a benefit

Does the title appeal to everyone?

No, and you don't care about everyone.

But for people who deal with hazardous waste, you will definitely enjoy knowing about this little gem.

This is your target audience, and it's your job to get them to read your ad. Your title is the way to do this.

Okay, now where do you find great headlines?

You look at other successful ads (especially direct response) that have stood the test of time. You look at the advertisements used regularly in magazines and other publications. How do you know they are good?

Because if they didn't do their job, the advertiser wouldn't keep placing them over and over again.

You sign up for the list of big direct response companies and save the emails.

Do you read celebrity magazines?

Celebrity magazines have some of the best headlines.

Pick up a recent edition and you will see what I mean. Okay, now how can you adapt some of these headlines for your own service or product?

The appearance of your title is also very important. Check that the type used is bold and large, and different from the type used in the text. Generally, longer titles tend to be better than shorter ones, even when targeting more "conservative" prospects.

This way you use other people's successful titles, but adapt them for your own product or service. Never copy a title (or any other piece of writing) word for word. Copywriting and advertising agencies are notoriously famous for prosecuting plagiarism. And rightfully so.

When More You Say,

The More You Will Sell

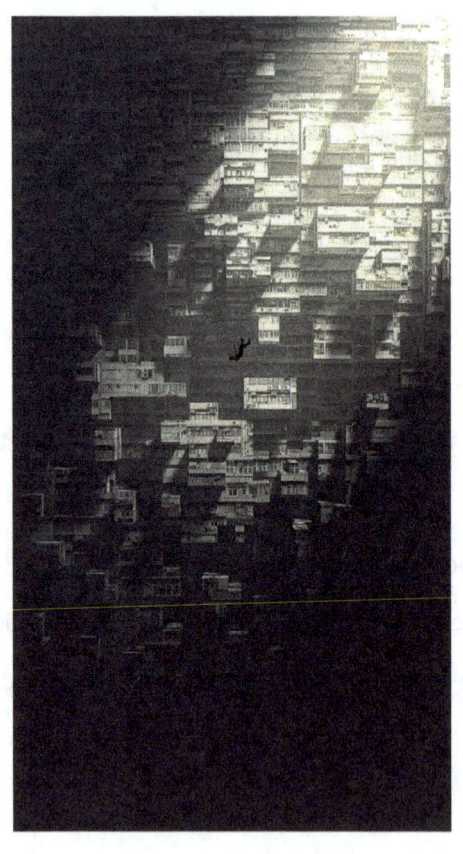

The debate about using long textsversus Short texts don't seem to have an end.

It's usually a newcomer to the world of copywriting who seems to think long texts are boring. They say "I would never read so many texts."

The fact is that all things being equal, long texts will always outperform short texts, and when I say long texts, I don't mean long and boring texts, or long and non-segmented texts.

The person who says they would never read the entire text is making a huge mistake in copywriting: they are following their gut reaction instead of trusting test results. She is thinking that he himself is the prospect. And she isn't. We are never our own prospects.

There have been many studies and tests on long texts versus short texts. And the winner is always the long text. But I'm talking about long, relevant text rather than boring, long, untargeted text.

Some significant research has found that reads tend to drop off sharply after 300 words, but don't drop off again until around 3,000 words.

If I'm selling an expensive set of golf clubs and I send my long text to a person who plays golf occasionally or has always wanted to try golf, I'm sending my sales pitch to the wrong prospect.

Not an effective target. And so, if a person who receives my long text doesn't read past 300 words, they are not qualified for my offer.

It wouldn't matter if you read up to word 100 or 10,000. They wouldn't make the purchase either way.

However, if I send my text to an avid golfer, who has recently purchased other expensive golf products through the mail, painting an irresistible offer, telling him how his game will improve in 10 strokes, he will probably read every word. And if I have segmented my message correctly, he will buy.

Remember, if your prospect is 3000 miles away, it's not easy for them to ask a question. If you want to be successful, you must anticipate and answer all your questions and overcome all objections in your text.

And make sure you don't throw everything you can think of into the text. You only need to include as much information as you need to make the sale... and not a word more.

If it takes 10 pages of text, so be it. If it takes a 16-page megalog, that's fine. But if in testing 10 pages sell better than the 16 page megalog, then use the winner.

Does this mean that every prospect must read every word of your copy before they order your product? Of course.

Some will read every word and then go back and reread it again.

Some will read the title and continue, jumping much of their body and landing at the end. Some will scan the entire body, and then go back and read it. All of these prospects could end up buying the offer, but they could have all different reading styles.

And that brings us to the next tip.

Write in a Scannable Way

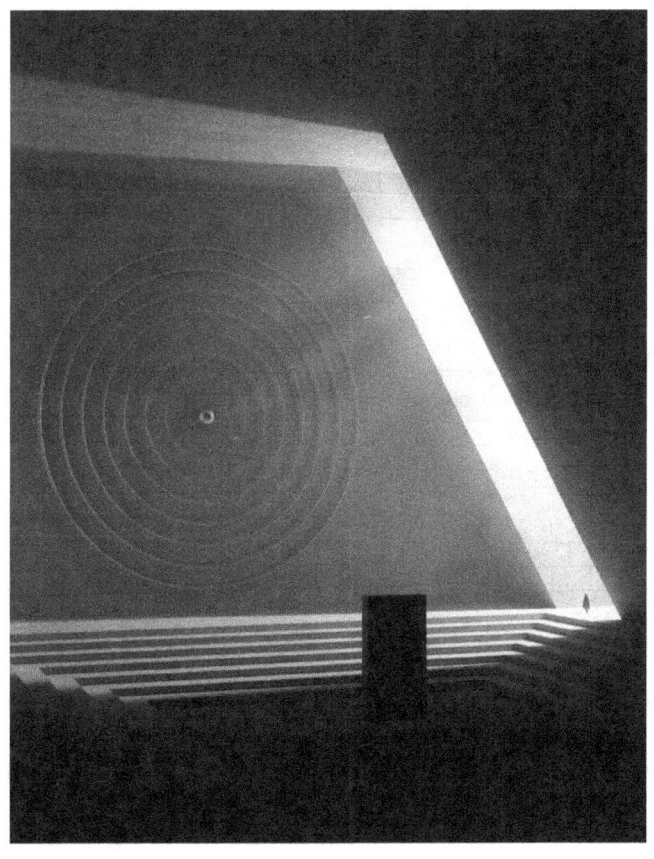

I just love formatsscannable, see the example below:

Suddenly

If I tell you a story

In this format

No accurate information

But with a high emotional charge...

Maybe you will be moved

Because the story is so vague

What could have happened to you!

But that

Hand passes

From a text

Made to manipulate your emotions

Saying a lot

Without saying anything.

Your layout is very important in a sales text, because you want your text to have an inviting look, refreshing for the eyes. In short, you want your prospect to stop what they are doing and read your text.

If he sees text with small margins, no indentations, no breaks in the text, no white space, and no subheadings...

If he sees a page, with words grouped densely, do you think he will be tempted to read it?

If you have white space with wide, generous margins, short sentences, short paragraphs, subheadings, and an italicized or underlined word here and there for emphasis, he will definitely be interested in reading.

When reading your text, some prospects will start at the beginning and read it word for word. Some will read the title and perhaps the subtitle, then read the "PS" at the end of the text and see who the text is from, and then start at the beginning.

Some people will skim the text, noting the various subheadings strategically placed by you throughout your text, then deciding whether it's worth their time to read the whole thing. Some may never read the entire text, but buy anyway.

You must write to all of them. Long, interesting and attractive text for the reader who likes details, and short paragraphs and sentences, white space, and subtitles for the jumpers.

Subheadings are the smaller headings spread throughout the text.

When you are in the process of creating a title, some of the titles that are not good enough will be good as subtitles. A subtitle forces your prospect to keep reading, captivating them from the beginning to the end of your entire text.

The Framework That Can Save You From Writer's Block

There is a well-known structure to successful sales pages, described by the acronym AIDA.

AIDA represents:

- Attention
- Interest
- Desire
- Action

First, you capture your prospect's attention. This is done with your title. If the ad fails to capture your prospect's attention, it fails completely. Your prospect doesn't read your star text, and doesn't order your product or service.

Then you build strong interest in your prospect. You want him to keep reading, because if he keeps reading, he might buy.

Next, you channel a desire. Having a target audience for this is key because you're not trying to create a desire in someone who doesn't have it. You want to capitalize on an existing desire that your prospect may or may not know they already have. And you want your prospect to want the experience that your product or service offers.

Finally, you present a call to action. You want him to pick up the phone, return the response letter, watch the sales presentation, order your product, or whatever.

You need to ask for the sale (or a response, if that's the goal). You don't want to beat around the bush at this point. If your letter and AIDA structure is solid and convincing, this is where you present the terms of your offer and want the prospect to act now.

Much has been written about AIDA formula copywriting. And I would like to add one more letter to the acronym: S for Satisfy In the end, after the sale is made, you want to satisfy your prospect, who is now a customer.

You have to deliver exactly what you promised (or even more), within the deadlines you promised, in the way you promised.

In short, you want to give him every reason in the world to trust you the next time you offer him a new offer.

And of course you want him not to return the product to you (although if he does, you must execute your return policy as promised).

Either way, you want your customers to be happy. They will make you a lot more money in the long run.

Learn how to Increase Urgency

When you limit the supply of a product or service in some way (i.e. limited sale), basic economics dictates that demand will increase.

In other words, people generally respond better to an offer if they believe the offer is about to become unavailable or restricted in some way.

And, of course, the opposite is also true. If a prospect knows that the product will be available whenever they need it, there is no need for them to act now.

And when your ad is put aside by your prospect, the chances of closing the sale greatly decrease.

So, your job is, to get your customers to buy, and buy now. Using scarcity to sell is a great way to achieve this.

There are basically three types of limitations:

1 - Limit the quantity

2 – Limit time

3 - Limit to offer

In the first method, limiting quantity, you are presenting a fixed number of products available for sale. When they're gone, it's over.

Some good ways to limit the amount include:

• Only have a number of units made

• Selling old stock to make room for new ones

• Limited number of items with cosmetic defects

• Only a number of products will be sold to avoid saturating the market.

• Etc.

In the second method, limiting time, the deadline is added to the offer. It should be a realistic deadline, not one that changes all the time (especially on a site, where the deadline appears to be close to midnight... when you come back the next day, the deadline has mysteriously changed to that day). Changing deadlines reduce your credibility.

This approach works well when the offer, or price will change, or the product/service will become unavailable, after the end date.

The third method, limiting the offer, is accomplished by limiting other parts of the offer, such as the guarantee, bonuses or prizes, prices and so on.

When using the limited sale, you must be sure to comply with the restrictions. If you say you only have 500 items to sell, then don't sell 501. If you say your offer will expire at the end of the month, make sure that happens.

Otherwise, your credibility will decrease. Prospects will remember the next time you throw another offer in their hands.

Another important thing you should do is explain the reason why the offer is being restricted. It is not enough to say that the price will rise in three weeks, but to explain why it will rise.

Here are some examples of limited sales:

"Unfortunately, I can only handle a limited number of clients. Once my time is full, I will be unable to accept any other business.

So, if you are serious about strengthening your investment strategies and creating more wealth than ever before, you should contact me as soon as possible. "

"Remember: you must act by [date] midnight in order to get my 2 bonuses.

These bonuses were offered by [third party company], and we have no control over their availability after this period. "

We only have 750 of these items from our supplier. Once they run out, we won't be able to get more until next year.

And even then we cannot guarantee that the price will remain the same. In fact, because of growing demand, it is very likely that the price will double or triple by then! "

Remember what I said earlier, people buy based on emotions, and then make their purchasing decision with logic. Well, using limited selling, the restriction becomes part of the buy-and-buy-now logic.

Whether you realize it or not, you now know more about

creating effective advertising than most of your competitors.

Want to prove it?

Ask them about any of the ideas we discussed. In response, you will likely receive wrong answers and blank stares.

That's because most of your competitors are too busy running their businesses to stop and

learn how to make them more successful. I congratulate you for doing so. In fact, the little-known tips, tricks, techniques, and principles I shared

with you here are the same as a marketing consultant

or advertising agency would use if you hired them for a lot of money. There's no reason why you can't use them and reap the best rewards.

Conclusion

Good copywriting is made, not born.

It's derived from proven test results designed to do one thing and do it well: Sell.

Effective advertising is not always "grammatically correct."

She uses short sentences and fragments.

Convince him to buy, and to buy now. Full stop.

Talk about benefits, not features. Sell the emotion in the ad and reinforce the decision to buy with logic.

Paint a compelling picture and have an irresistible offer that compels your prospect to act and act now! And if it doesn't, then you don't have any interest in the ad.

Effective persuasion is like your top salesperson who continues to break records for all their sales for the year, multiplied by thousands or millions!

Imagine if this seller, the only one with proven results, could be multiplied as many times as you would like.

That's effective marketing!

This is the proven type of marketing you need to use.

I wish you great results from now on.